Walk Around

A Suburb

Peter and Connie Roop

Heinemann Library
Des Plaines, Illinois

Designed by Lindaanne Donohoe
Printed in Hong Kong

03 02 01 00 99
10 9 8 7 6 5 4 3 2 1

Library of Congress Cataloging-in-Publication Data

Roop, Peter.
    A suburb / Peter and Connie Roop.
      p.   cm. — (Walk around)
    Includes bibliographical references and index.
    Summary: Describes the housing, schools, transportation,
recreational opportunities, shopping, and other aspects of life in
the suburbs, using Rancho Bernardo, California, as an example.
    ISBN 1-57572-130-9 (lib. bdg.)
    1. Suburbs—United States—Juvenile literature. [1. Suburbs.]
I. Roop, Connie. II. Title. III. Series: Roop, Peter. Walk around.
HT352.U6R66 1998
307.76'0973—dc21

98-14934
CIP
AC

Acknowledgments
All photographs by Phil Martin except those listed below.

Cover photograph: Phil Martin

The author and publishers are grateful to the following for permission to reproduce
copyright photographs:
© First Image West, Inc./Reed Kaestner, p. 4 (Brisbee); Robert Whitmore, p. 5 (Edison).

Special thanks to Bob Smith, R.S.V.P. Administrator and Ray Wilson, Principal, Westwood
Elementary School, Rancho Bernardo, California.

Every effort has been made to contact copyright holders of any material reproduced
in this book. Any omissions will be rectified in subsequent printings if notice is given
to the publisher.

Some words are shown in bold, **like this.** You can find out what they mean by looking
in the glossary.

For Heidi, who helps wherever she is.

Contents

What Is a Suburb?

Rancho Bernardo, California

Brisbee, Arizona

A suburb is a **community** near a big city. It is part of a **metropolitan area.**

Just under half of all people in the United States live in suburbs. All suburbs are different, but they have some things in common.

Gurnee, Illinois

Edison, New Jersey

Mapping the Suburb

A suburb is not as crowded as a city. Places in a suburb are spread out. Most people use cars to get around in the suburb. Some people in the suburb may use **public transportation** to get to a large city.

This map shows Rancho Bernardo, California, the suburb you are walking around in this book. Rancho Bernardo is part of the San Diego **metropolitan area.** About 40 thousand people live in Rancho Bernardo. About one million people live in San Diego. People in Rancho Bernardo can take Highway 15 to get to San Diego and use Rancho Bernardo Road for short trips.

Rancho Bernardo

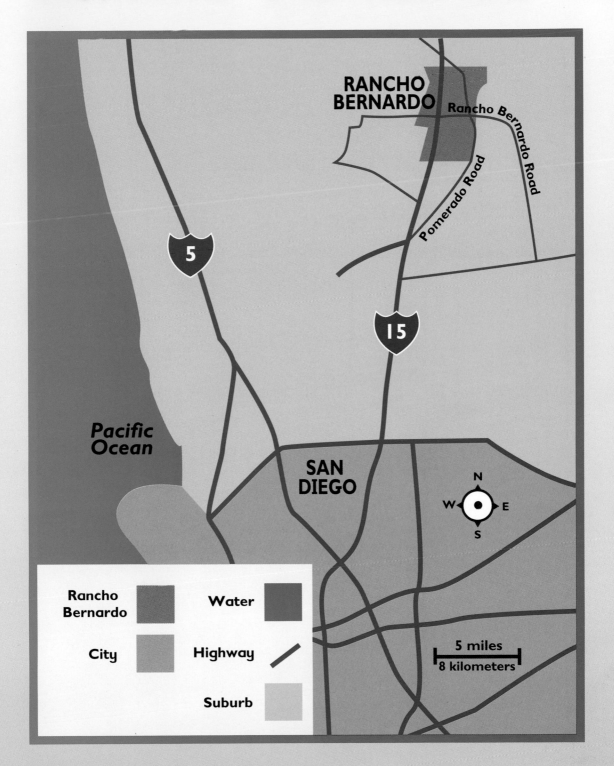

RANCHO BERNARDO

Rancho Bernardo Road

Pomerado Road

5

15

Pacific Ocean

SAN DIEGO

N
W · E
S

Rancho Bernardo

City

Water

Highway

Suburb

5 miles
8 kilometers

Homes

Most homes in a suburb are houses. Many have garages and yards. Some people live in apartments or **town houses.** Instead of garages, apartments have parking lots.

Many apartments have **balconies** and play areas that are shared. Houses and apartments are in **neighborhoods.** There are many neighborhoods in a suburb.

Getting Around

Many people in a suburb take buses, trains, or other kinds of **public transportation.** Most people drive cars to get around a suburb. Unlike in a city, many places in a suburb have large parking lots.

For short trips or to get around traffic,
many people walk or ride bikes.

Schools

Most schools in a suburb are one or two stories tall. They have large playgrounds. There are many schools because many families with kids live in the suburb.

Many children ride to school in buses.

Others walk or ride bikes to school if it is

in their **neighborhood.**

The Police

There is usually one police station in a suburb. Many officers work there. Most police officers **patrol** the suburb in cars.

This suburb also has **volunteer** police officers. Some officers help the **community** by working or speaking in schools and other places.

Working

Some people work in a large city but do not live there. Many people live in a suburb near the city. They **commute** to work using **public transportation** or cars.

Many people live near where they work because it is easy to get to their jobs. They work in offices, factories, and stores in the suburb. Many people help build the homes, buildings, and roads in the suburb.

Shopping

People drive cars in the suburb to do their shopping. Stores have plenty of parking. People shop at **strip malls** and big shopping malls along busy roads.

People who live outside the suburb also shop at large malls in a suburb. Suburbs have big supermarkets where people buy food. These stores stay open late at night so people who work during the day can shop, too.

The Library

The suburb has a large library where people borrow books. There may be more than one **branch** of the library. It may be part of a large city, **county,** or state library system.

This library has thousands of books. People use computers to find things in the library.

Banks and Money

There are many banks in a suburb. These banks have drive-up windows so people can do their banking as they wait in their cars. People can also get money from cash machines in stores and shopping malls.

The Post Office

A post office in a suburb is big. There are many workers to help people with their mail. Most mail is brought to homes by letter carriers.

People drive cars to the post office to mail letters and special packages. They can park easily to go inside or they can use the drive-up mail boxes near the post office.

Playing

Children play outside in their **neighborhoods** with their friends. When the weather is bad, they play indoors. Inside, children play video games, watch TV, or make up their own games.

Suburbs have parks, playing fields, and movie theaters. Many people go into the large city to visit museums, zoos, and **aquariums,** and to see plays or listen to music.

Helping Out

In a suburb, there are many different **neighborhoods.** People work together on projects such as helping people in need and keeping the **community** clean.

Many people pick up trash and **recycle.**
Others take care of buildings and clean
parks and empty lots. Neighborhoods
working together help people feel like they
belong to the community.

Glossary

aquariums places with fish and underwater animals

balconies small porches that stick out from buildings

branch smaller part of something bigger

community area where people live, work, and shop

commute to travel from home to work and back

county areas that states are divided into

metropolitan area area that includes a large city and its surrounding suburbs

neighborhoods small areas of a city, town, or suburb in which homes, streets, and other things are alike

patrol to guard or watch an area

public transportation ways of travel that are organized and that everybody can use

recycle to collect paper, plastic, cans, and glass so that they can be used again

strip malls long buildings divided into many different stores

town houses many homes connected together

volunteer to help someone or do a job without being paid

More Books to Read

Around Town. New York: DK Publishing, 1995.

Burton, Virginia. *The Little House.* New York: Houghton Mifflin, 1998.

Coster, Patience. *Towns & Cities.* Danbury, Conn: Children's Press, 1998.

Fitzpatrick, Shanon. *Communities.* Cypress, Cal: Creative Teaching Press, 1995.

Gutman, Bill. *In Your Neighborhood.* New York: Henry Holt & Company, 1996.

Robinson, Lynn. *A Street Called Home.* Orlando, Fla: Harcourt Brace, 1997.

Index

6900